Iranian Regime's Nuclear Duplicity

An Analysis of Tehran's Trickery in Talks with the P 5+1

NATIONAL COUNCIL OF RESISTANCE OF IRAN
US REPRESENTATIVE OFFICE

IRANIAN REGIME'S NUCLEAR DUPLICITY;
An Analysis of Tehran's Trickery in Talks with the P 5+1

Copyright © National Council of Resistance of Iran - U.S. Representative Office, 2016.

First published in 2015 by
National Council of Resistance of Iran - U.S. Representative Office (NCRI-US)
1747 Pennsylvania Ave., NW, Suite 1125, Washington, DC 20006

ISBN-13: 978-0-9904327-5-3
ISBN-10: 0-9904327-5-3

Library of Congress Cataloging-in-Publication Data

National Council of Resistance of Iran - U.S. Representative Office.
IRANIAN REGIME'S NUCLEAR DUPLICITY; An Analysis of Tehran's Trickery in Talks
with the P 5+1

1. Iran-Military policy. 2. Nuclear weapons-Iran. 3. Iran-Foreign relations. 4. Security,
International. 5. Rouhani, Hassan.

First Edition: June 2015
Second Edition: January 2016

Printed in the United States of America

CONTENTS

Iranian Regime's Nuclear Duplicity

An Analysis of Tehran's Trickery
in Talks with the P 5+1
June 25, 2015

Executive Summary

International negotiators have been engaged in talks with the Iranian regime on its nuclear program since 2002. The current approach, led by the United States as part of the so-called P5+1, is now in its final stages. While opinions may vary as to the contents and wisdom of the deal that may be taking shape, all understand that the success of any agreement will be dependent on whether the Iranian regime can be trusted to curtail its decades-long quest for a nuclear weapon. As President Obama has suggested, if this agreement results in Iran becoming a nuclear power, history will judge the signatories harshly and it will evaluate whether they acted based upon factual evidence regarding the Iranian regime's past and current behavior.

This book examines Iran's behavior throughout the negotiations process in an effort to inform the current dialogue on a potential agreement. Drawing on both publicly available sources and those within Iran, the report focuses on two major periods of intense negotiations with the regime: 2003-2004 and 2013-2015. Based on this evidence, it then extracts the principles and motivations behind Tehran's approach to negotiations as well as the tactics used to trick its counterparts and reach its objectives.

Ultimately, the reader is left with one inescapable conclusion:

The Iranian regime has deliberately capitalized on the illusion of "building trust" to counteract and defuse necessary and indispensable "transparency" requirements that would make up the critical components of any successful nuclear agreement.

Evidence in the report to support this conclusion includes the following:

- **"Building Trust"**

  o Verbal promises and commitments to international negotiators regarding only the already-disclosed information (not concealed activities);

  o Falling back on the alleged, but undocumented, 2003 "fatwa" attributed to Supreme Leader Ayatollah Ali Khamenei against developing or pursuing nuclear weapons.

- **"Transparency"**

  o Demand for immediate relief from international sanctions with no prior commitment to disclose the full history of Iran's nuclear program;

  o Refusal to meaningfully answer 11 outstanding

IAEA questions related to the military aspects of the program, and refusal to allow international inspectors to access sensitive military sites, individuals, and related documents.

This report reveals that Iranian negotiators continue to firmly stick to the playbook and ground rules established by Khamenei and other senior officials since 2002. By professing an eagerness to "build trust," which the evidence overwhelmingly suggests is disingenuous and rather deceitful, Tehran seeks to foster a sense of misplaced hope and optimism among its interlocutors. Regrettably, after more than a decade of war in the Middle East, P5+1 leaders appear to think that Tehran is genuine in its intentions, which simply flies in the face of facts, but is perhaps in accordance with domestic political objectives or the perception that the current approach averts another war.

However, before they sign on to an agreement that will certainly be judged by historians in the near future and will have significant consequences for the region and beyond, we recommend they review the findings in this report and ask themselves if Iran's actions have demonstrated a true commitment to transparency about their past and current nuclear program. Only a positive answer can form the basis of an agreement that can be relied upon to protect the region and the world from one of its most critical threats.

Iran's Guiding Principles and Modus Operandi in Nuclear Negotiations

Overview:

Since August 2002, when the National Council of Resistance of Iran (NCRI) unveiled the Natanz uranium enrichment and Arak heavy water reactor sites, Tehran has been engaged in several rounds of negotiations with international counterparts regarding its controversial nuclear program.

The following analysis, unique in many respects, relies on a combination of sources within the public domain as well as within the Iranian regime. It uncovers and explains Tehran's negotiating tactics as well as the guiding principles behind those tactics.

There is broad consensus that Tehran, especially in the past two years, has entered the talks out of desperation and weakness as a result of the pain caused by international sanctions. The nuclear program, one of the hallmarks of Tehran's attempts at projecting power in the past 25 years, has now become a cause of weakness and has placed the regime at a strategically devastating deadlock. Ali Khamenei, the regime's Supreme Leader has agreed with the talks fearing another extensive public uprising that would further destabilize the regime.

Throughout the negotiations period, Khamenei has personally overseen the process and he has set and articulated all the main contours and guidelines.

Tehran's dominant attitude in the negotiations:

The overall framework that Khamenei has dictated, and which regime senior officials have agreed to, is that the talks must only focus on known sites, projects and aspects of the nuclear program – the existence of which cannot be refuted anyway. In the meantime, the entire infrastructure, especially the weaponization aspect and its various branches, must remain intact, and out of the scope for the talks. This topic should be marginalized as much as possible and turned into a secondary and insignificant issue in the talks.

This is the most crucial, significant, and determining component of Tehran's approach in the talks.

Khamenei has personally defined and articulated the framework for the nuclear talks for the negotiating team. While he has publicly revealed some aspects of the regime's framework, including the scope of enrichment to be carried out in Iran and the lifting of sanctions, a review of Khamenei's positions and in particular the red lines laid out by him, three themes stand out and have been consistently reiterated by him over the past two years:

- *No access to military sites*

- *No access to Iranian nuclear scientists*

- *Refusal to halt nuclear research and development*

These themes constitute the main pillars of the military aspect of the Iranian nuclear program. In other words, for Khamenei, the main red lines intend to preserve and safeguard the most crucial and fundamental aspects of the nuclear weapons program, and he has implied this time and again.

Tehran's systematic exploitation of the illusion of "Building Trust" to neutralize necessary and indispensable "Transparency" measures

One of Tehran's core practices in the negotiations process has been its emphasis during the past two years on "building trust." It has especially given verbal guarantees of cooperation while referring to an undocumented fatwa attributed to Khamenei (allegedly banning the use of nuclear weapons).

The aim of the regime is to marginalize "transparency" requirements while avoiding the provision of information regarding its real objectives, particularly the possible military dimensions (PMD) of its program. The regime has consistently obstructed attempts to gain insight into its past activities, has refrained from offering concrete answers to serious questions, and has attempted to minimize or indefinitely suspend investigations. Instead, Tehran has fostered an illusion that it is building "trust" through other means, such as verbal promises and references to an elusive religious decree against nuclear weapons.

Tehran's approach in the past two years vis-à-vis the IAEA has been telling and supports the suspicions outlined above.

During this period, despite numerous marathon talks, the IAEA has not made much progress in addressing a host of unanswered questions regarding the PMD of the regime's nuclear program. Tehran has only been transparent in its refusal to provide answers to the IAEA's serious questions while restricting further access for the UN watchdog in the past two years. As a result, the IAEA has not been able to make significant headway on 11 key areas regarding the PMD aspects.

Khamenei's fatwa: a ploy to build trust

One of the main arguments advanced by the clerical regime as a means of "building trust" in lieu of concrete "transparency" measures, has been a constant reference to an alleged fatwa by Khamenei, declaring that Weapons of Mass Destruction in general and nuclear weapons in particular are forbidden.

Javad Zarif, the regime's chief nuclear negotiator and foreign minister, has cited the purported fatwa repeatedly during the talks as one of the main reasons that the regime's nuclear program does not have a military nature.

The regime's officials assert that this fatwa can be ratified and become legally binding. Prior to his trip to New York and during his speech at the UN General Assembly in 2013, the mullahs' president Hassan Rouhani once again underscored the fatwa as proof that the regime's nuclear program is peaceful.

The purpose of this mysterious fatwa, however, is to simply deceive the international community. It is standard practice for all fatwas to be handwritten, bear an official stamp, and distributed via the press or official websites. But, there has never been any written declaration banning nuclear arms in Khamenei's handwriting, or bearing his official stamp.

Aside from such technicalities, even if the fatwa existed, not all prohibitory fatwas are binding for the government or its officials. Except for the fact that Ali Larijani, the Speaker of Majlis (parliament) stated on October 31, 2013: "The leader has declared the use of nuclear weapons as haram (prohibited)." Officials choose their words carefully in this regard, and it is clear that the expression "declared *haram*" is not necessarily a binding decree for the regime or its senior officials.

A prominent Islamic scholar, Ayatollah Jalal Ganjei,[1] has written a detailed review of reports on the fatwa in the context of Islamic jurisprudence, arguing that the fatwa, even if exists, would have little value since the credibility of a fatwa may be assessed on three grounds: its correctness, utility, and the competence of the one who issues it. The strength of a fatwa largely hinges on the religious expertise of the person issuing it, and Ali Khamenei is not considered a jurisprudent in Iranian and Shiite religious centers.

Ganjei further reasoned that first, a fatwa is only binding for the followers of the religious scholar who issues it, and any officer or commander who follows another religious scholar or considers

---

1   Ganjei, Chair of the Commission for Freedom of Religion and Denominations of the National Council of Resistance of Iran was a pupil of Khomeini's in Najaf when he was in exile and subsequently stood up against Khomeini's religious dictatorship, earning himself a death sentence and branding as an infidel but he escaped Iran.

himself outside the scope of the decree, is not obligated to follow it. In addition, there is no punishment for failing to adhere to a fatwa.

Second, and more importantly, any fatwa issued by anyone may be declared void by "secondary decrees." The most imperative cases that give rise to "secondary decrees" are "emergency circumstances."

Ayatollah Ganjei elaborated that as far as the Shiite jurisprudents involved in the regime are concerned (including Supreme Leader Ali Khamenei and his predecessor and founder of the regime, Ruhollah Khomeini), *Jawaher al-Kalam* (a 50-volume collection written by Sheikh Mohammad Hassan Najafi in 1850) is considered to be the only credible source of Islamic jurisprudence. *Jawaher al-Kalam* quite clearly states, "In the course of the battle with the enemy, it is permitted to stage a siege, prevent anyone from entering or leaving; use catapults, guns, gunpowder; rain down deadly and poisonous snakes, scorpions and other deadly animals; destroy walls and houses; cut off trees; rain down fire and cause floods [to the enemy's site]; and anything else that would increase the chances of overpowering the adversary." In another section of the text, the author writes, "Poisoning the enemy's water or food is considered 'haram' by some... and is reluctantly accepted by others... But if this is the only way to defeat the enemy, it is permitted without qualification."[2]

Accordingly, the use of weapons of mass destruction in the view of the clerics ruling in Iran is permissible and so Khamenei's informal rejection of nuclear weapons cannot be a basis for the *haram* classification unless it is done for a different objective (deceiving the enemy as they claim), to be superseded at a later stage when it is deemed necessary.

---

2   *Jawaher al-Kalam* (Beirut, 1981), pages 66-67.

This shows that what is being touted as a religious decree issued by Khamenei is anything but that, and the fatwa is simply a lie meant to deceive the West (the enemy) in order to achieve a clear state objective.

The Context:

This report reviews two major periods in the West's intense negotiations with the Iranian regime (2003-2004 and 2013-2015). It outlines seven principles that define Tehran's approach as well as eight tactics used to reach the regime's ultimate objectives.

For the past 12 years, Tehran and the international community have been engaged in talks over Iran's disputed nuclear program. These negotiations, mainly conducted with the EU3 (France, the UK and Germany) or the P5+1 (the EU3 plus the U.S., China and

Russia)), have been among the longest running talks in modern history. They have continued with various levels of intensity.

Negotiations in search of an ultimate solution to the nuclear issue were first launched a few months after the revelation of the clandestine uranium enrichment site at Natanz and the heavy water reactor at Arak in August 2002 by the National Council of Resistance of Iran (NCRI).

Now, after many rounds of talks, starting with the EU3 and continuing with the permanent members of the UN Security Council plus Germany (P5+1), the international community is at a critical juncture. A dozen of these rounds of talks have taken place in the last 20 months alone.

However, the diplomatic approach has shown little concern in way of understanding the forces and motivations governing Tehran's behavior. In addition, the factors that determine Tehran's reaction and attitude in the talks have undergone major changes.

The Key Question:

Is Tehran pursuing a well-defined strategy and specific tactics, or have its tactics been adapted to various circumstances?

What evidence-based conclusions can be drawn from dozens of rounds of talks when it comes to Tehran's modus operandi and observable behavior?

An analysis of probable answers to these questions, which have not received sufficient scrutiny, may be especially helpful at this stage, as Western powers try to assess Tehran's positions and actions under a tight self-imposed deadline.

This report, based on research and studies conducted by the US Representative Office of the National Council of Resistance of Iran, is the first of its kind and attempts to probe Tehran's objective in the talks, along with its methods and tactics.

Hassan Rouhani, key and unique individual in Iran's nuclear program

Iranian President Hassan Rouhani has played a significant and rather unique role in Tehran's nuclear program and in the talks that have taken place over the years, beginning long before his presidential tenure in 2013.

Until 2005, Rouhani was secretary of the regime's Supreme National Security Council (SNSC), which was established in August 1989 as the highest decision-making body on national security matters. Not surprisingly, the nuclear dossier has been under the purview of this state decision-making organ. Rouhani has thus been involved in all policy discussions surrounding the nuclear program as well as in the execution of all its vital projects.

On October 6, 2003, subsequent to international concerns raised after the exposing of the clandestine aspects of the nuclear program, Supreme Leader Ali Khamenei ordered Rouhani to personally assume responsibility of the nuclear case. He thus became the head of the team negotiating with the West. He held this position until August 2005 when the administration of then-President Mahmoud Ahmadinejad took office.

After Ahmadinejad became president, Rouhani remained at SNSC, where he worked as Khamenei's representative. Today, as the president of the Islamic Republic, he heads the Supreme National Security Council. Rouhani has thus played a key role in the nuclear file. There are very few officials in the regime that can claim to have the extent and depth of knowledge and information about the regime's nuclear program.

Setting aside the negotiations over the past 20 months and the November 2013 interim agreement, nuclear talks with Iran only led to results in another period, namely with the Tehran Declaration of 21 October 2003 and the Paris Declaration of 15 November 2004. In both cases, Hassan Rouhani headed the negotiations with the EU3 (France, Germany, and Britain).

In light of this, Rouhani's conduct, perspectives, and positions reflect to a great degree, the conduct, perspectives, and positions of Tehran and the system that is pursuing the nuclear project.

SOURCES (PUBLIC AND CLASSIFIED)

This report reviews and assesses the conduct of Tehran's negotiating team during the various stages of the negotiations and evaluates Tehran's approach and observable reactions during the talks. The report relies on four different categories of sources.

Public sources:

- *National Security and Nuclear Diplomacy*: This book is effectively Rouhani's memoirs for the period of 2003 to 2004, during which time he was in charge of the nuclear dossier. Rouhani published his account of the period in this 1200-page book in autumn 2011. This is the first book by a senior regime official covering the period when Rouhani headed the nuclear negotiations.

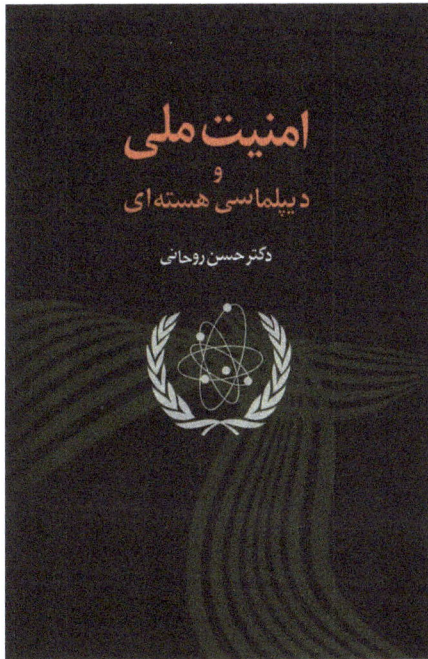

- **Rouhani's speech before the Supreme Cultural Revolution Council (SCRC) on November 3, 2003:** When Rouhani was responsible for Iran's nuclear file, he gave an in depth speech at the Supreme Cultural Revolution Council (SCRC), briefing regime officials on the issue. Entitled "Beyond Iran and IAEA challenges in the nuclear file," the text of the speech was later published in the autumn

2005 edition of *Rahbord* magazine, a quarterly run by the Expediency Council's Strategic Research Center, which has Rouhani himself as the editor-in-chief.

Classified sources:

Two classified reports by the Office of Political and Legal Studies of the Majlis (parliament), both dated December 2004, shed further light on the hidden aspects of the tactics and assessments leveraged by the Iranian regime in its negotiations with the West. These reports, which have not been made public, are:

- **"Substantive study of Tehran and Paris agreements – Report No. 1"**
- **"A critical and analytical look at the Paris Agreement – Report No. 2"**

The reports were prepared in December 2004 to brief legislators on the nuclear talks.

Copies of the documents have been obtained by the National Council of Resistance of Iran (NCRI), a coalition of democratic opposition figures and organizations, from inside the Iranian regime. They include aspects of the regime's internal assessments regarding the nuclear talks.

Main Findings:

Despite the changing formats of the negotiations over the years or the various individuals leading the talks with the West (four individuals under three presidents), a study of the negotiations shows that as far as Tehran is concerned, certain basic tenets are constantly at play and Tehran has been pursuing specific objectives all along. This study has ascertained seven fundamental principles governing the Iranian regime's position:

Basic Tenets:

1. **Supreme Leader as the Ultimate Decision Maker:**

   Decisions are made at the highest levels of the Iranian regime. In practice, the negotiating team advances the strategy dictated by the regime's leaders, in particular the Supreme Leader Ali Khamenei. The composition of key decision-makers on the nuclear program has not changed significantly over the past two decades. Saeed Jalili, the principal negotiator during Ahmadinejad's era, is among the special advisors to Khamenei in these negotiations.

2. **Evade Addressing Military Dimensions:**

    As far as Tehran is concerned, the military dimensions of the nuclear program should be marginalized as much as possible. They have either never been discussed or intentionally minimized and watered down. Military sites have in principle been excluded from inspections. In the few exceptional cases where access has been granted, inspections have been fully controlled, limited, opaque and specifically designed to simply get rid of the issue at the negotiating table.

3. **Only Address Disclosed Sites:**

    The talks or agreements already reached have only touched on the publicly disclosed aspects of the nuclear program. Tehran has never shown any desire to reveal all aspects of its program. In fact, the opposite is true. The Iranian regime has consistently attempted to claim that the program has already been made public in its entirety and that there is nothing else to disclose.

4. **Delay Addressing IAEA Concerns:**

Tehran has tried to cover the program, dodge offering necessary responses to queries, create ambiguity, and leave IAEA questions unanswered. It has only offered semblances of a reply when left with absolutely no other option. Even then it has only given the absolute minimum information just to escape further scrutiny.

5. **Preserve the Entire Nuclear Infrastructure:**

As far as Khamenei is concerned, every attempt must be made to preserve the nuclear program in its entirety. In particular, research and development has not ceased at any juncture.

6. **Build Trust Verbally:**

Where serious issues have been raised about the program, the Iranian regime has offered verbal promises and attempted to gain trust by using already disclosed secrets while concurrently postponing and not responding to IAEA investigations.

7. **Keep the Talks Alive:**

Resorting to and showing a constant inclination for negotiations have been employed as tactics by Khamenei to prevent the international community from adopting a resolute policy vis-à-vis Iran. The aim is to continue the nuclear program under the guise of negotiations. On the other hand, Tehran is also reluctant to find itself in a position where the talks reach an impasse since this would pave the way for the adoption of a resolute policy by the international community.

TEHRAN'S MAIN NEGOTIATING TACTICS

This study shows that Tehran has consistently employed at least eight major tactics to achieve the above-mentioned goals:

1. Buy More Time:

Buying time and prolonging the negotiations

Amongst the principal methods specified by Khamenei to be employed in the talks has been to buy more time and prolong the negotiations. Tehran calibrated the negotiations in such a way that without offering anything specific in return, the negotiations would continue, or any breaks in the negotiations would be short lived.

2. Avoid the PMD:

Distracting attention and focus from the possible military dimensions of the program, pushing it to the margins, and delaying concrete responses

A tactic continuously employed by Tehran to prevent investigations into the essence and ultimate objective of the nuclear project, has been to moderate the role of the military figures and their presence in the decision making apparatus of the program. Not only has Tehran refused to bring up such matters, it has also through various tactics attempted to deny the issue altogether. As an example, Tehran and in particular Rouhani never clarified the role of IRGC Brigadier General Ali Hosseini-Tash, Deputy Defense Minister between 2003 and 2004, who attended meetings at the Supreme Nuclear Committee. Although these were minister-level meetings (and in the case of the Atomic Energy Organization of Iran, AEOI, only the head of this organization attended), surprisingly, the Deputy Defense Minister accompanied the Minister. According to detailed information, the organ tasked with weaponization of the nuclear project (i.e. SPND headed by Dr. Mohsen Fakhrizadeh) was working under Hosseini-Tash at the time.

3. **Prevent Access to Sensitive Sites:**

   Tehran has consistently either refused or stonewalled IAEA access to sensitive sites.

4. **Hide until Exposed:**

   Refusing to provide information or transparency regarding projects, smuggling networks, or illicit measures until disclosures and revelations are made by other sources (constant emphasis by the regime that the whole project and its dimensions have been disclosed and there is nothing left to report on).

   One of the principal tactics used by Tehran in the talks is that it would only offer the least possible amount of information necessary to keep the negotiations alive. The Iranian regime offers information only when it is absolutely necessary to do so or when credible and undeniable information reaches the IAEA or parties to the negotiations from other sources.

5. **Defer to Lengthy Reports:**

   Deferring answers until lengthy reports are prepared and pertinent authorities have studied those reports

   Tehran has on several occasions bought more time at various junctures by presenting "comprehensive and detailed reports" or even by simply making promises about reports "that would explain everything and would clarify all issues". This is a clear delay tactic to kick the can down the road and avoid transparency for as long as possible.

6. **Inject Optimism:**

   Encouraging the perception that negotiations are bearing fruit in order to extract more concessions down the road

Tehran often persuades its counterparts that the talks are making progress and gaps are being bridged as a way to encourage optimism and extract further concessions.

7. Avoid Halting R&D:

Removing the issue of research and development from discussions

Tehran has always insisted that research and development is not up for discussion. This is one of the major evasions created and maintained by Tehran in the talks. To keep open the path to the advancement of its nuclear program, Tehran always haggles about the context of research and development as a method to continue such activities. As such, it has constantly kept its nuclear program on the march and this program has never been brought to a complete halt.

8. Talks on the Sidelines of Negotiations:

Attempting to resolve outstanding issues or reach deals with just one party in the talks on the margins of the negotiations and then confronting others with a fait accompli

Tehran would then use the deal as leverage to advance its position instead of resolving the core issue in the context of collective negotiations. It presents the deal reached on the margins of the talks as something agreed to by all parties and warns that opposition to it would derail the main course of negotiations.

FACTS AND CASES

1. Buying Time:

Hassan Rouhani, *National Security and Nuclear Diplomacy*, pages 392 and 393:

Excerpts of Rouhani's assessment as the Secretary of the Supreme National Security Council, March 2005:

It is important that we make moves so that time is on our side. Time can work in our favor when it comes to the issue of dealing with IAEA and the legal aspects of the case; and it may even lead to the termination of the case. Concerning the technological aspect, we must also move in a manner so that the passage of time will not be detrimental. Now for the next few months (to implement the necessary measures) the passage of time will not affect us, but after we have the necessary tunnels created, have moved the equipment underground in Natanz and have completed the shortcomings in Isfahan (the Uranium Conversion Facility to convert yellowcake into uranium oxide and uranium hexafluoride) that is when the passage of time can hurt us. From that point on the extension of the negotiations can become a burden for us in technological terms. On the other hand, putting an end to the talks and diplomatic efforts will not be in our favor so we have to explore other avenues.

Supreme Leader Khamenei, November 3, 2013:

God willing, we shall not suffer losses from these negotiations and the nation will gain experience that much like the experience of temporary suspension of enrichment during the years 2003-2004, it will advance the intellectual and analytic capacity of the people... a decade ago, in the negotiations with Europeans, we accepted some sort of retreat or suspension that was compulsory. However, after two years of suspension and closing down of many activities, we all learned that even through such steps we absolutely cannot hope for any cooperation from the Western counterparts... Had we not done so, some might have claimed that had we once retreated, the problem would have been solved and the nuclear file would have turned normal. However, with the experience of temporary suspension, everyone understood that our counterparts are after something else; thus we restarted the work and the progress.

Office of Political and Legal Studies of Majlis to the Parliamentary Office for Political and Legal Studies:

The Islamic Republic of Iran, like other governments that succeeded in obtaining nuclear technology, must use a zigzag approach (suspension + no suspension) and alternating strategies (coercive diplomacy and reconciliation), to be able to succeed in our national determination to bring nuclear science home and to fully obtain it.

Office of Political and Legal Studies of Majlis – 2nd Report- page 11

The main goal of the Islamic Republic of Iran at this time should be that the government must see the time remaining as the last opportunity for completion of work on uranium enrichment and the nuclear fuel cycle.

Rouhani speech as SNSC Secretary:

We need to stall and buy time in order to transform potentialities into actualities. If one day we are able to complete this cycle, the world will be faced with a fait accompli, thus changing the whole equation.

...

We will continue the negotiations with the Europeans for a few months and in the worst-case scenario we will reach the situation that we are in today. The minimum outcome will be delaying Security Council measures. If we had to go to the Security Council in November, (by engaging in negotiations) we will delay this for at least another year... During this period we can work on completing our technology.

Sirous Nasseri, a senior member of Iran's negotiating team in Mohammad Khatami's government, regarding the negotiations with EU3, (*ILNA* state run news agency, June 13, 2015):

…The most difficult, important and decisive part of the technical operation in the enrichment and production of nuclear fuel is related to the basic UF6 material… The day we succeeded in producing the UF6 -- I think we stockpiled around 40 tons -- that day we discovered that we had a good bargaining chip. Regarding the other arenas, for example regarding Arak, we offered no commitments.

ANA News Agency
Photo: Mohammadreza Abbasi

Mohammad Saeidi, former AEOI Deputy for Programming, International and Majlis Affairs who resigned from his post in December 2009 and since the onset of Iran's nuclear file was a permanent member in the negotiations (*ILNA* state run news agency, June 13, 2015):

…If for a certain period we voluntarily accepted the Additional Protocol it was because we wanted to advance our nuclear program effectively and in peace. If we accepted voluntary suspension for a certain period, it was because we wanted to preserve the nuclear program itself.

Office of Political and Legal Studies of Majlis – 2nd Report, page 1:

The Paris Agreement on Nov 15, 2004 (between Iran and the EU3), like the Declaration of Tehran on Oct 21, 2003, was a successful attempt at diplomatic negotiations and continuous bargaining on our end.

Hassan Rouhani, National Security and Nuclear Diplomacy, page 132:

At that point, it was believed that in negotiating with Europe (EU3) we could largely neutralize the role of the United States. The purpose of negotiating with Europe was first to gain enough time to complete different components of our nuclear program and second to convince them that we are not trying to build a nuclear bomb and that continuation of enrichment in Iran according to the rules of the NPT should be accepted and conceded to.

Hassan Rouhani, National Security and Nuclear Diplomacy, Pages 150 and 151:

In a letter to the regime's leaders, Rouhani presents his proposals on the regime's objectives in negotiations with EU3 foreign ministers:

If our nuclear dossier is referred to the Security Council, what will be on the table will not be limited to the issue of sanctions or to a military strike with a limited possibility, but rather more importantly our nuclear achievements may be at risk..... Our strategy must be multifaceted to "preserve the achievements of the country's nuclear program and its completion", "avoid referral of the dossier to the Security Council", and "transform threats into opportunities"... If someday we have to go to the Security Council we must arrange for the preparations beforehand.

Hassan Rouhani, National Security and Nuclear Diplomacy, Page 155:

Therefore, at the first meeting of the Supreme Nuclear Committee, upon accepting the responsibility, I pointed out the views of the Supreme Leader on Oct 6, 2003 so that all members would be aware of their responsibilities…

The second topic of discussion was around suspension. The decision was that we have to manage the suspension in a manner so that we can reach a possible agreement with Europe while completing our nuclear technology. Our red line on suspension was systems whose technologies had not yet been completed (we had to manage in such a way so that they would not be suspended).

Hassan Rouhani, National Security and Nuclear Diplomacy, pages 360-361(elaborating on the operational plan for the period of suspension):

Hassan Rouhani laid out in December 2004 the operational plan for the suspension period:

The suspension period is an opportunity to resolve the problems … so that when we restart, we will not be faced with delays in the production process. Briefly, these are the steps that need to be followed during the suspension period:

- Completing the gas production process for storage of UF4 at Isfahan

- Removing the glitches of UF6 production and raising the quality of the product

- Completion of the UO2 program and its facilities

- Creating a section for residuals that did not exist before

- Preparing a safe and secure place to store the products

- Continuation of research to overcome defects and improve the quality of research, and future planning

- Problem solving for possible underground floor vibrations at Natanz, which can lead to explosion of the centrifuge units used for enrichment

- Careful and confident planning in the shortest time possible to launch a series of 164 unit cascades of centrifuges

- Parallel and independent follow up of the P2 program (more advanced centrifuges), which is the ultimate and long-term objective of the enrichment program

- Completing the Arak heavy water production in the shortest possible time.

Hassan Rouhani, National Security and Nuclear Diplomacy, Page 280:

At a meeting with senior officials on the 25th and 26th of September 2004, I submitted a report concerning the technological developments in the past year and I pointed out that with the continued work of UCF in Isfahan this chapter was closed. Activities at the Natanz underground facility had not come to a halt for a second and continued nonstop; also in Arak, all activities continued without interruption...."[3]

Hassan Rouhani, *National Security and Nuclear Diplomacy,* **Pages 454 and 455** *(ending suspension immediately after becoming confident regarding enrichment capability, April 2005)*

I always believed that whenever we became confident of our enrichment capabilities, we would put an end to the suspension. It was only for this reason that we accepted suspension of enrichment voluntarily for a short period of time. In a few letters to the heads of the three branches, I pointed out that we need several tons of UF6 before we can start our enrichment process; moreover we have to complete our technology and we will have to transfer the materials and the equipment to a safer place (tunnels).

The main goal of our diplomatic activity was first and foremost to create an opportunity to complete our technology and to increase our country's ability for enrichment. The second reason was confidence-building and resolving allegations and suspicions. I had repeatedly told the head of the Atomic Energy Organization of Iran (AEOI), if he could start a pilot program of 164 centrifuges in cascade in a two-month period and acquire a 3.5% enrichment yield that would be the day we would cease the suspension immediately.

At a meeting where several of the experts had been called to participate so they would get into discussions with the experts

---

3   This is the period that Iran's nuclear program was supposed to be suspended based on an agreement with the EU3

of the AEOI, the experts asserted that even 8 months from now AEOI will not be able to launch a pilot program. They provided their technical reasoning. The conclusion of this meeting was sent to the heads of the three branches of government. If we wanted to break the suspension and not be able to reach our goals within about 5 months it would have been a lose-lose situation. The AEOI record was not reliable and we could not count on their analysis because prior timelines were superseded with longer delays.

2. Avoiding the PMD:

Fereydoun Abbassi Davani, head of Atomic Energy Organization of Iran (AEIO) from March 2011 to June 2013, *ISNA* News Agency, September 5, 2011:

They resorted to propaganda regarding my background in the Islamic Revolutionary Guard Corps (IRGC). There were some concerned people in the country that said it would be best if IRGC members do not get involved in this kind of activity. But why? Are the colleagues in the IRGC foreigners? The IRGC is the protector of the Islamic Revolution. Given the fact that during the years of war the assets of the country were in general and in their various aspects also concentrated in the hands of the IRGC, it would only be rational to use this [IRGC] potential in every facet of the country.

Ali Khamenei, June 24, 2015:

Even during the years of restriction, research and development must continue. They say that we should do nothing for 12 years, but this is double the bullying and double the audacity... I am absolutely against unconventional inspections and interrogation of figures as well... We shall not accept inspection of military centers as we have previously said so... We are against a delay in the implementation of the other party's commitments and making it conditional to an IAEA report. This is because the IAEA has on many occasions proven that it is not independent or just; we thus don't trust it. They say that the "IAEA should be assured"; this is an irrational statement. How could it be assured unless it inspects every inch of this territory?

Ali Khamenei, May 27, 2015:

The other point that I touched upon speaking to the respectable officials and I am telling this to you as well is that under no circumstances, under the pretext of supervision, should they infiltrate the security and defensive sanctity of the country; absolutely not. The military officials of this nation are not allowed in any manner to permit foreigners to enter the security and defensive sanctity and bulwark of the nation, under the pretext of monitoring, under the pretext of inspections, and such.

...The next point is that no unconventional monitoring of the Islamic Republic that makes this a unique country in the sense of monitoring is allowed under any circumstances. The same supervision that is the norm in the world should also be here as well but nothing more.

...Last point in this regard is that the scientific and technical nuclear development in its various aspects should not be halted under any circumstances. Development ought to continue; technical development. It could be that they [regime's officials] may deem necessary to accept some restrictions; that is alright with us. Go ahead and accept some restrictions, but certainly technical development must continue and advance with full force.

Ali Khamenei, May 20, 2015:

...As stated before, permission for any inspection of military centers or talking with nuclear scientists or scientists of other sensitive branches and insulting their sanctity shall not be granted.

...I shall not allow foreigners to come and talk and interrogate the scientists and the dear and prominent children of this nation. The brazen adversary expects that we allow them to talk to our scientists and scholars about a fundamental indigenous and

national progress, but such permission shall never be granted...
the adversaries of the Islamic system and all those who are waiting
for decisions by our system should clearly take note of this matter.

Hassan Rouhani, National Security and Nuclear Diplomacy, page 141

The Defense Minister was present in the Supreme Nuclear
Committee. Likewise, a representative from the Defense Ministry
participated in the meeting of experts. Moreover, Mr. Hosseini-
Tash would also participate in the Supreme Nuclear Committee
meetings.[4]

Sirous Nasseri, a senior member of Iran's negotiating team in Mohammad Khatami's government, regarding the negotiations with EU3, ILNA State run news agency, June 13, 2015

With respect to answering the questions about the possible
military dimension (PMD) of Iran's nuclear program:

The U.S. and the P5+1 will either concur or not concur that we
are going to do nothing about the illusory [PMD] allegations. I
think that if we do nothing, they have to get along with us.

---

4   IRGC Brigadier General Ali Hosseini-Tash, Deputy Defense Minister,
     has been overseeing the weaponization of the nuclear project.

Mohammad Saeidi, former AEOI Deputy for Programming, International and Majlis Affairs, who resigned from his post in December 2009 and was a permanent member in the negotiations since the start of the nuclear crisis, ILNA State run news agency, June 13, 2015

...It is not so that Iran inevitably has to agree that the resolution of PMD is a precondition to a deal. We need to arrive at an agreement with them regarding the framework of a peaceful nuclear activity and this issue can also be a matter to be discussed and resolved between Iran and the IAEA sometime in the future.

Hassan Rouhani, National Security and Nuclear Diplomacy, pages 146-147

Another problem arose from the fact that we had not declared to the IAEA the facilities we had set up in Natanz, the material we had imported, the construction of centrifuges, and above all, the injection of the nuclear material, which had been carried out without notifying the agency, a fact further corroborated by IAEA studies. Still worse, in the sampling done at Natanz they had learned that there is contamination of up to 79% in Iran; a matter that deeply worried the West. They thought that Iran was not telling the truth and that there are clandestine sites in this country for enrichment for military purposes.

Another concern of the IAEA was that some of the parts were being manufactured in companies affiliated with the Defense Ministry. The IAEA analysis was that in the first stage the military was involved in the enrichment and it was in the later stage that non-military elements partook. In early November 2003, I traveled to Vienna, where ElBaradei [former head of the IAEA] told me in a private meeting that he had information that due to the imposed war[5] and the threat of Saddam using WMD, these activities were first initiated in the military sector but were abandoned after the end of the war. He told me that if we make such an announcement, he would take care of the nuclear file. He proposed that we say: "Since we were at war and a dangerous enemy such as Saddam was pursuing WMDs, in order to defend ourselves, we were compelled to go after enrichment, but we abandoned it after the war." He stated that if we say this, the whole thing will blow over. ElBaradei stated: The evidence and information presented by the West involves a certain period, namely when you had to do it, and then you naturally abandoned it. I reacted harshly and told him that such statements are fictitious and without foundation. I said that he had accepted these baseless allegations due to U.S. and Western inductions. He responded that perhaps I was unaware that the military involvement in the nuclear project was taking place. I told him nothing could take place regarding the nuclear issue in Iran without my knowledge. I was an official during the war and after the war I was responsible for the security of the country. Never have our military men sought to enrich uranium.

3. No Access to Sensitive Sites:

Hassan Rouhani, National Security and Nuclear Diplomacy, pages 212-213

---

5   Iran-Iraq war in the regime's terminology

Image credit: DigitalGlobe - ISIS
Image date: January 30, 2005
Farsi writing that says "Chemi Daroo"
Centrifuge research and development facility

For a long time they (IAEA) wanted to inspect Kala-Electric. From the time they placed the request to the time permission was granted several months had passed. Kala-Electric was the first site where enrichment was carried out using centrifuges, but had not been reported to the IAEA. Thus, it was very important for the IAEA to inspect it. Apparently our specialists were technically unaware of the new IAEA instruments. Basically, if nuclear activity has been conducted at a site, its traces will never be gone. Even the neighboring buildings and trees will be contaminated. Usually they take samples from inside the air ducts or air conditioning systems or the seams of the walls. They would wipe a cloth there and send it to the lab. If a trace of contamination remained, that would have been incriminating enough to establish guilt. The instruments we possessed showed nothing, but the cloth they wiped there and sent to some industrial countries, the result was announced in 45 days. The sensitivity of their instruments were several hundred times that of ours. A case that became problematic for us was a 36% contamination in one of the rooms of Kala-Electric. In the ensuing months, we had the issue regarding higher contaminations (such as 80%) resolved but this case remains unresolved. Judging by the type of contamination they stated that it was the residue of a reactor and given its specifications, it probably belonged to a former Soviet republic.

Hassan Rouhani, National Security and Nuclear Diplomacy, page 261 [Denying permission for the inspection of Defense Ministry workshops]

Another excuse expressed by the Europeans was that we would not allow the IAEA to inspect Defense Ministry workshops and they couldn't know if the production of parts and their assembly has also been suspended in the military sector or not.

Hassan Rouhani, National Security and Nuclear Diplomacy, pages 211-212

In inspection of military sites, as anticipated in the Additional Protocol, they had to observe certain rules, which were later put in ink as regulations. They needed to use vehicles with window curtains when they entered military sites so that they would not be informed of other facilities near the one they had come to inspect. They should not carry instruments that identify geographical coordinates (GPS) or have their mobile phones with them. They needed to hand over all their personal belongings at the entrance of the military site. The military personnel were told that if the inspectors wanted to enter a hall, they should cover everything there with drapes since they were just allowed to take samples. Thus they needed to show on the map which site they wanted to go to and then they had to identify the specific hall in the satellite pictures and only then could they take samples of the place. In the early days, we went easy on them. However, at one point in a meeting of leaders concerns were raised, and observance of the above framework was emphasized. For example, if IAEA inspectors saw a machine manufactured by a certain country, they would pressure that country to cut off its trade with Iran. Thus we emphasized that the machines be covered up. In fact a decision was made to strictly adhere to the framework set by the regulations. Therefore, the relevant regulation was prepared by the Defense Ministry and was later circulated.

4. Hide until Exposed:

Hassan Rouhani, National Security and Nuclear Diplomacy, page 120:

In 2002 our activities went on in a quiet, calm, and serene ambiance but suddenly under the order of the United States, the Hypocrites [Tehran's derogatory term to refer to the Iranian opposition, the People's Mojahedin Organization of Iran, the MEK] through a press conference made a lot of unfounded accusations and created a lot of noise....

Rouhani speech as SNSC secretary:

One of the members of the Supreme Council of the Cultural Revolution had stated that [the nuclear project] had to be conducted in secret. We meant to keep it a secret, however it was revealed by spies. This project was not meant to be made public.

...

The story behind the discovery of the Natanz site is that the Hypocrites [MEK] contributed to its discovery. They had different sources of information and collected information from various sources. They were informed of some of the comings and goings in the Natanz area. They had realized something was going on there. They had even gotten very close, photographed the site and collected information.

....

We had hidden some of our activities and thought no one was aware of their existence.

....

(In response to a question from a member of the Supreme Cultural Revolutionary Council on whether the regime had lied to the IAEA about P2 centrifuges, Rouhani responded: No, we have not lied... of course in some cases there might have been a delay in declaring things).

Hassan Rouhani, National Security and Nuclear Diplomacy, page 262

The P2 issue was a challenge. The IAEA asserted that we had purchased the drawings for the P2 centrifuges in 1994, yet we claim had not started working on the P2 until 2001. The IAEA asked about what we did during the 7 years? How could a country purchase the drawings and not work on them for 7 years? Another problem was that the engineer who worked on the P2 production claimed that he got his technical orders from the head of the Atomic Energy Organization of Iran. IAEA asserted that the head of the AEOI is not tech savvy so he could not have given him the orders. IAEA wanted to know the technical group that supposedly supervised him and issued the orders to him. The AEOI insisted that there is no other body, but the IAEA would not accept this claim.

...

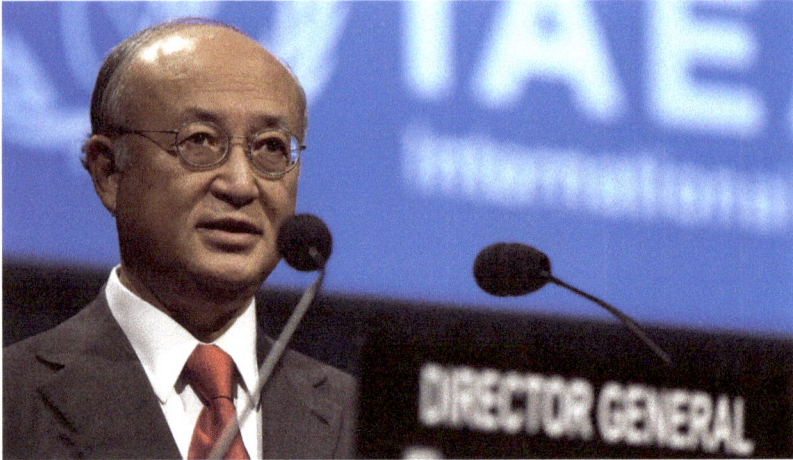

In a meeting with [IAEA Director General] Mohamed El-Baradei, he claimed that 7,000 pieces of P2 have been lost on the black market and it is unclear to which country they have been shipped. Several P2 parts were in Libya but upon receiving them IAEA realized that 7,000 of them were missing. They claimed that these parts must be in our possession and we responded that we have not purchased any P2 parts. Thus, two problems (the missing 7,000 parts and the 7 year gap) as well as failing to report the purchasing of the drawings and the purchase of a large number of magnets from abroad for the P2 to the IAEA were some of the main causes of complexity with the P2 issue.

Hassan Rouhani, National Security and Nuclear Diplomacy, pages 162-164

El-Baradei [in his private meeting with Hassan Rouhani] added: I am bewildered as to what to do with AEOI. I am perplexed. At one point the organization used to say that its technology is indigenous; then after much investigation, it said that in 1995 it had 70,000 pieces imported. Later on it stated that some of these pieces had entered Iran in 1985. Then it claimed that under no circumstances has anything been injected into the centrifuges. But later during discussions it became clear that injection had taken place. With such a climate of distrust, how can we trust this organization? I am glad that you are now responsible for this file. I hope that you will put an end to this. Until you give us a complete picture of all your nuclear activities, we cannot make any remarks. You are producing UCF in Isfahan and the AEOI says that it is building it without any pilot. How can it be that a country would spend so much on a factory without any pilot projects? They tell us that material has not been injected, but experts concur that what is observed in Natanz is impossible to achieve without prior test of nuclear enrichment.

Hassan Rouhani, National Security and Nuclear Diplomacy, Pages 233-235

Subsequent to the implementation of the Tehran Agreement and the issuance of the November 2003 resolution and signing of the Additional Protocol in December of the same year in Vienna (by Dr. Salehi, representative of Iran in IAEA), the internal and external commotion had subsided to a large extent. Then, suddenly, it was reported that the existence of P2 centrifuges had not been declared in the AEOI report to the IAEA, which was supposed to be "accurate and complete." As such, the Europeans and the IAEA claimed that the organization's report had not been accurate and complete. In the meeting of experts, when the AEOI was asked why P2 had not been noted in the report, it replied that it had acquired the P2 diagram from the Internet and thus there was no need to report it.

Following the crisis that had unfolded, we thought it was imperative that we travel to Vienna to talk to IAEA officials. In the lengthy meeting that I and the negotiating team had with El-Baradei and his deputies on January 7, 2004, in the residence of Iran's representative to the IAEA, ElBaradei expressed great concern and discontent regarding the situation and noted that in the next meeting of the IAEA Board of Governors Iran will not be in a good position and that we have regressed to the conditions prevailing in September [2003]. He then explained about the developments in Libya and concluded that we had bought the P2 design and drawings from a dealer and had failed to report it. Additionally this has not been mentioned in the AEOI's report. Similarly, in the following days, the Europeans told our experts in a meeting that either Mr. Rouhani had been informed about the P2 and said nothing or he had not been informed. They elaborated that in the first case, this has damaged the mutual trust between us and in the second case his stature in the country has been damaged.

El-Baradei also told me that this matter has dented the confidence building process. I told him that I did not believe it was a matter of any significance, but he replied that this matter was of great importance: The dealer has sold the same diagrams and equipment that to you that he has sold to the Libyans and Libya has handed everything over to the United States. Of importance was the fact that Iran's credibility in the IAEA and EU3 and even the whole West had been badly damaged. ElBaradei noted that the case was not limited to that, and that we had also failed to report the Polonium (neutron source)[6]. In the end, I told him that we will look into these issues and get back to him.

…The Libyan development proved troublesome for me because the dealer that we had purchased the centrifuges from was the same individual who had sold the centrifuge and other equipment to Libya. In fact, Libya had unmasked all dealers in the black market and passed on their information to the U.S. and U.K. We were entirely in the dark that Libya had surrendered to the West and had given them all its nuclear equipment and information.

As I mentioned, when we reported our nuclear activities to the IAEA (October 2003), in a handwritten and private letter to El-Baradei we had declared that we had bought the centrifuges from a dealer and that we did not know his nationality, but that he looked Indian and he identified himself as Taher. At the time, we did not know that the IAEA had obtained precise documents on this dealer from Libya.

---

6   In addition to various functions, polonium is also used in the detonation of a nuclear bomb.

Rouhani's speech as SNSC secretary:

We have not named Pakistan anywhere yet. We have said that we bought it from a dealer. We even told them that our primary dealer was a European. They asked us about the nationality of this Mr. Taher that has made a deal with us and we replied that he looks to be from the sub-continent.

Hassan Rouhani, National Security and Nuclear Diplomacy, page 236[7]

During my trip to Vienna (in January 2004) and in the course of negotiations with IAEA officials, the fact that the above issues were brought up by the AEOI was completely new and concerned us. We had scarcely reviewed the intricacies of the November resolution concerning the discussions of Libya, the sale of P1 and P2 designs and pertinent machines [centrifuges], as well as the transfer of drawings for the nuclear bomb to Libya by a dealer who called himself Taher, which raised doubts on the part of the IAEA and Europe regarding Iran's nuclear file. In any case, it became clear that Libya had handed over all its equipment and information to the U.S. and the IAEA. Moreover, Taher had been arrested in Malaysia and had seemingly confessed that in the 1990s he had handed over the P2 drawings and blueprint to Iran in Dubai in exchange for $3 million.

---

7   The regime's contract with the dealer of P2 centrifuge diagrams is exposed.

At the outset, the AEOI would not confirm this and in response to the insistence of the IAEA declared that the P2 diagrams, along with the P1 centrifuges and the relevant documents, were given to Iran without AEOI requesting them and that no extra money had been paid for them. IAEA officials pointed to the fact that it is downright impossible that we had bought the P1 centrifuges and the sellers would have given us the P2 design for free. Ultimately, the Atomic Energy Organization of Iran admitted that it had purchased the P2 designs in 1995.

Rouhani speech as SNSC secretary:

On the P2 issue, we told IAEA that there were activities in a small workshop of the private sector and nowhere else. They have not yet accepted this. IAEA asks have we spent so much money to get these designs and blueprints only to give the designs to a person to work on them in a small workshop? They allege that we are conducting the real work at another site.

Hassan Rouhani, National Security and Nuclear Diplomacy, page 231

During the discussions around UCF with the IAEA, the disappearance of some UF4 and its conversion to uranium metal turned into an issue. Despite its previous denial, the AEOI admitted to it in its statement of October 2003 and it was registered as an activity carried out in the 1990s. Uranium metal was a sensitive matter for the IAEA since it could be used for the outer layer of a bomb.

Hassan Rouhani, National Security and Nuclear Diplomacy, pages 231-232 [plutonium and polonium]

The next point concerned plutonium where the IAEA stated that Iran had reprocessed close to 7 kg of UO_2 using hot cell and subsequently separated plutonium. Following the October statement, the IAEA conducted inspections, announced the discrepancies of the report presented by Iran with the IAEA findings and questioned the statement. Of course, the AEOI had announced the existence of plutonium in its statement. Thus, the discrepancy was just over the quantity. Ultimately, however, the issue was resolved. Another issue that raised much tumult was that of polonium that had not been declared in the statement.

Hassan Rouhani, National Security and Nuclear Diplomacy, page 264 [laser enrichment]

Of the above mentioned, what was more important was our 15% laser enrichment. We had stated that we had carried out experimental laser enrichment for the amount of 1 mg. In its sampling, the IAEA concluded that Iran had enriched up to 15% using lasers. The IAEA opened a piece and took it to Vienna for testing and discovered that it was 15% contaminated which showed that an accurate report had not been provided in this regard.

Hassan Rouhani, National Security and Nuclear Diplomacy, p 238 [confessing to falsifications on the leak of UF6]

The claim of the leak of UF6 from the cylinders damaged the credibility of AEOI and ultimately AEOI had to admit that the material had been used and injected into the centrifuges. Later, during samplings at Kala-Electric and also when the material was accounted for it became evident that injection had been carried out.

Hassan Rouhani, National Security and Nuclear Diplomacy, page124 [high enrichment contaminations]

The outcome of the tests conducted in March 2003 by taking samples in Natanz was announced by IAEA in June 2003 and it was determined that in the study of samples from Iran, traces of highly enriched uranium had been discovered. The study showed contaminations of 79%, 75%, 54%, and 20%. The agency even stated that it had discovered 79% enrichment and thus Natanz was probably a façade and Iran most likely developed other secret sites. Iran's representative at the agency travelled to Tehran to report the case and he explained the outcome of the samplings in the meeting of the Supreme Nuclear Committee. Everyone was astounded. Some argued that this was the work of IAEA itself and that tools that had been used for the sampling must have been contaminated. No one believed that such a high contamination level, indicative of weaponization aspirations, could have been found in Iran. The officials of AEOI also offered no logical explanation and they simply questioned the authenticity of the tests.

5. Defer to Lengthy Reports:

Hassan Rouhani, National Security and Nuclear Diplomacy, page 243 [a 1,000-page report to cover up a number of issues]

In the meeting, I bragged about a 1000-page report to cover up some of the issues that had been brought up. Ultimately, ElBaradei promised that he would do his best so that his report for the March 2004 Board of Governors session would be suitable.

Hassan Rouhani, National Security and Nuclear Diplomacy, page 237

In my meeting with ElBaradei in January 2004, he told me that if this trend continues, Iran's file will most likely be referred to the UN Security Council. At the same time, the Europeans sent messages about a breach of commitments on our part. Thus, after December [2003], we were facing a critical situation. We were having a hard time in those days. I told ElBaradei to calm things down to give us time to study things and offer the appropriate response. The agency said that it knew the building, room and even which desk drawer the polonium (neutron source) report was in. Thus, the Western countries had plenty of information about

AEOI. The IAEA had even declared to the relevant officials the exact place of the polonium documents.

6. Inject Optimism:

Office of Political and Legal Studies, 2nd Report:

Signing the Paris Declaration between Iran and European governments… increased Iran's political maneuvering power and this in turn increased our bargaining power with the IAEA and governments involved in the negotiations.

7. No Halt to R&D:

Ali Khamenei, July 7, 2014

…Research and development should surely be preserved.

Ali Khamenei, April 9, 2015

Everyone should take note that despite the negotiations the activities of the Islamic Republic of Iran concerning nuclear research and development shall not be halted under any circumstances and none of the nuclear achievements may be lost. Additionally, the relationship between the International Atomic Energy Agency and Iran should be conventional and not extraordinary.

Of course, conducting negotiations should not be interpreted in a sense that the Islamic Republic of Iran will abandon its nuclear science progress... the nuclear science progress should not be halted or even slowed down... none of the country's nuclear achievements may be closed down... if scientific progress in nuclear technology continues firmly and in earnest, achievement of a variety and spectrum of technologies will swiftly follow; thus, regarding the progress in the nuclear science there is no ground for any halt or slowing down.

Mohammad Saeidi, former AEOI Deputy for Programming, International and Majlis Affairs, who resigned from his post in December 2009 and since the start of Iran's nuclear crisis was a permanent member in the negotiations, *ILNA* **state run news agency, June 13, 2015**

...The importance of the research and development achievements is more than the number of machines [centrifuges]. I am saying this from a technical perspective. I also said this to Dr. Zarif prior to the Lausanne negotiations that if you can extract the right of research and development from the P5+1, it would be splendid and fortunately, in addition to research and development, we also got 5,060 spinning machines.

Hassan Rouhani, National Security and Nuclear Diplomacy, page 155

The second topic of discussion was around suspension. The decision was that we have to manage the suspension in a manner so that we can reach a possible agreement with Europe while completing our nuclear technology. Our red line on suspension was systems whose technologies had not yet been completed (we had to manage in such a way so that they would not be suspended).

Rouhani speech as SNSC secretary:

Another issue was that the Europeans gradually came to the conclusion that we had only accepted the suspension in the areas in which we had no difficulties. In areas where we had technical difficulties we had not accepted the suspension. They actually pointed this out to us during the negotiations. The Isfahan UF6 plant, which converts yellowcake to UF4 and UF6 was completed during the period of suspension. When we were talking to the Europeans in Tehran we were still installing the necessary machines and we had a long way to go before the completion of the project. In the relaxed atmosphere that was created we managed to complete the project in Isfahan.... And now we are able to convert yellowcake to UF4 and UF6 and that is a very important matter.

8. Side Talks:

Rouhani speech as SNSC secretary:

We presented ElBaradei with a text about that dealer and the equipment we had purchased from him in a private and separate paper as an attachment to the complete report that we had presented to the IAEA.

Hassan Rouhani, National Security and Nuclear Diplomacy, page 166

(A private meeting with ElBaradei) – ElBaradei expressed concern about the high contamination. As the person responsible for the security of the country, I assured him that never has there been a high level enrichment in the country and the contaminations were due to contaminated parts that had come from abroad. However, he had a hard time believing it. He hoped that ultimately what I had stated would be right.

Hassan Rouhani, National Security and Nuclear Diplomacy, page 208-209

Basically, in the Tehran Agreement it was decided that Iran would present a comprehensive picture of its program to the IAEA. This matter was consistently worked on in AEOI until the report was finally prepared.

Experts at the foreign ministry were somewhat skeptical about the report that had been prepared by the organization and told me it is not clear how thorough the report was. I went ahead and asked the head of the organization whether the report was thorough. He stated that the report was indeed thorough and the topic that was not addressed was the issue of the dealer and receiving the parts in Dubai. I consulted the negotiating team if they thought ElBaradei ort, but that in a private and handwritten letter we write about it to ElBaradei and tell him that on a certain date in Dubai, the organization had made a deal with a dealer that we don't know his nationality and that he had introduced himself as Taher and might be of Indian origin. After the Tehran talks, this was the first practical step to report to the IAEA on 18 years of activity. Europeans in return had promised that they would prevent propaganda on the issue once the report had been presented.

The Way Forward

Recommendations:

In order to close all paths of the Iranian regime to the nuclear bomb, something that has on numerous occasions been claimed by the Obama administration to be the ultimate goal of the negotiations, the following steps are imperative and essential and they ought not to be negotiated away:

- Unconditional and immediate access to all known or suspicious sites (and those would could be revealed at a later date) that are suspected of being involved in the nuclear project, including all military, security and non-military sites;

- Unconditional and immediate access of IAEA to all scientists and experts involved in the nuclear program;

- Complete and unambiguous answers to all IAEA questions and investigations about the PMD of Tehran's nuclear program;

- Disclosure of relations and transactions with other countries, including North Korea, with respect to the nuclear and ballistic missiles programs;

- Immediate removal of all enriched uranium from Iran (except for the 300 kg agreed upon) in any form or shape it may be in;

- Tehran should come clean and it should provide all documents and previous work, including illicit networks and smuggling routes for purchasing nuclear equipment parts and technology;

- Ratification and implementation of the Additional Protocol;

- Lifting of sanctions should be conditional on complete "transparency" and providing comprehensive answers and granting full access to the IAEA; and

- The full implementation of the Security Council resolutions.

APPENDIX

Notable Nuclear Revelations of the Iranian Resistance

(1991-2015)

Since 1991 the Iranian resistance has exposed more than a 100 secret nuclear projects of the Iranian regime. Some of the more notable nuclear revelations include:

1. Revealing the regime's preliminary nuclear facilities in Mo'alm Kalaye (1991);

2. Revealing the attempt to purchase nuclear warheads from Kazakhstan (1992), the revelation aborted the shipment of the warheads to Iran;

3. Continuous revelation of hiring Chinese, Russian and N. Korean experts and the regime's teams travelling to these countries over the years on dozens of occasions;

4. Revealing the uranium enrichment facility in Natanz, being the

largest and most expansive of the regime's investment on its nuclear weapons program. The site was exposed on August 14, 2002 in Washington, DC, and disrupted Tehran's nuclear calculations and led IAEA inspections to Iran that confirmed the revelation;

5. Revealing the heavy water project in Arak (August 14, 2002) in a press conference in Washington, DC;

6. Revealing the most important companies involved in producing and importing equipment and necessary material for nuclear projects (February 2003 and August-September 2013), including Kala Electric in Aab-Ali highway that was registered as a watch-making factory. However, this was actually a center for centrifuge assembly and testing, and in an IAEA inspection, traces of highly enriched uranium was found at this site;

7. Revealing the Lavizan-Shian Center (May 2003). This was a very sensitive nuclear site for the regime and the mullahs immediately destroyed it and even removed the soil before allowing a June 2004 IAEA visit to the site;

8. Revealing the Lashkarabad site and its front company (May 2003). This site was inspected by the IAEA (October 2003), and the regime deceived the inspectors by taking them to another location;

9. Revealing in November 2003, the special role of the IRGC in the nuclear projects clearly showed the military goals and aspects of this project;

10. In April 2004, the NCRI revealed that Tehran had dedicated 400 nuclear experts to military industries;

11. Exposing the new Center for Readiness and New Defense Technology (Lavizan-2) in April 2004. The equipment and activities from razed Lavizan site was moved to this site, but the site was kept off limits;

12. In September 2004, NCRI revealed the allotment of $16bn to

nuclear technology, purchase and smuggling of Deuterium from Russia, as well as details on the AEOI's companies;

13. Revealing the Hemmat Missile Industries site in relation to produce nuclear chemical warheads (December 2004);

14. Revealing a project in February 2005 aimed at producing polonium-210 and beryllium to build nuclear bomb fuses;

15. Revealing the secret nuclear center in the Parchin tunnel (March 2005). This site focused on laser enrichment;

16. Revealing the production and importing graphite necessary for nuclear bomb production (May 2005);

17. Revealing the import and production of Maraging steel to build the bomb fuselage and using it in centrifuge systems (July 2005);

18. Revealing the production of 4,000 ready-to-install centrifuges (August 2005);

19. Revealing in a press conference in Washington, DC, in August 2005, the meeting between Abdul Qadeer Khan, and commanders of the Iranian Revolutionary Guards in 1986 and 1987 in Tehran;

20. Revealing in Brussels the regime's plans to smuggle tritium from South Korea to increase nuclear explosion power (September 2005);

21. Revealing, in a Washington, DC, press conference, the regime's tunnel construction in its military centers to keep secret the material and equipment (September 2005);

22. In a Washington, DC, press conference in November 2005, NCRI revealed that Iran was building nuclear capable missiles in underground secret tunnels;

23. Revealing the construction of an underground site near Qom (Fordow) in December 2005;

24. Revealing importing of industrial press machines to shape enriched

uranium in a bomb (January 2006);

25. Revealing the production of P2 centrifuges (August 2006);

26. Revealing in Washington, DC, the reactivation of laser enrichment projects (September 2006);

27. Revealing the specifications of 7 nuclear front companies related to the nuclear fuel cycle (February 2007);

28. Revealing a secret tunnel being constructed by the Ministry of Defense south of the Natanz site (September 2007);

29. Revealing the location of nuclear warhead construction in Khojeir and the nuclear weapon command center in Mojdeh (February 2008);

30. Revealing Beheshti University as a nuclear research center related to commanding weapons production in Mojdeh (March 2008);

31. Revealing Center of Explosion and Impact Technology (METFAZ) and changes in the nuclear command center (September 2009);

32. Revealing further details about the Fordow site (October 2009);

33. In September 2010, in Washington, D.C., the NCRI revealed a covert nuclear site located in tunnels in Behjatabad in the Abyek Township of Qazvin Province. This covert nuclear site was codenamed "311" and is known as Javadinia 2;

34. In April 2011, the NCRI revealed in Washington, DC, the covert site near Tehran, named TABA, which was involved in production of centrifuge parts for tens of thousands of centrifuges. Tehran conceded the existence of this site the next day;

35. Revealing in Washington, DC, in July 2011, the Defensive Innovation and Research Organization (SPND) nuclear bomb command center chaired by Mohsen Fakhrizadeh. SPND was later sanctioned by the Department of State in August 2014;

36. Revealing 100 names of nuclear engineering experts active in various bomb making sections (January 2012);

37. Revealing in Washington, DC, further details of SPND operations, its involvement in the Fordow site, and the list of experts associated with this center (April 2012);

38. Revealing the top-secret Maadan Sharq nuclear site in Tehran's Damavand district. (July 2013);

39. Revealing the relocation of Defensive Innovation and Research Organization (SPND) nuclear bomb command center (October 2013);

40. Revealing the "012" secret site in Isfahan's Mobarakeh linked to SPND (November 2013).

41. In a Washington, DC conference, revealing the Iranian regime's activities related to high explosive chambers at Parchin military site (November 2014);

42. Revealing in a press conference in Washington, DC, the existence of Lavizan-3 underground nuclear site in Tehran used for advanced centrifuge testing and research and development (February 2015).

43. Revealing the cooperation between the Iranian regime and North Korea regarding the nuclear weapons program of Iran and the presence of North Korean nuclear scientists in Tehran (May 2015).

44. Revealing Iran's deceitful tactics during nuclear negotiations with the P 5+1 (June 2015).

45. Revealing Iran's cooperation with North Korea to deceive IAEA inspectors (September 2015).

46. Revealing how Iran laid out a plan to deceive the IAEA in its probe of Possible Military Dimensions of Iran's nuclear program (December 2015).

www.ingramcontent.com/pod-product-compliance
Lightning Source LLC
Chambersburg PA
CBHW041301040426
42334CB00028BA/3118